Time flies over us, but leaves its shadow behind.

-Nathaniel Hawthorne

Also, by Bill Arnott

Gone Viking – *A Travel Saga*

Dromomania – *A Wonderful Magical Journey*

Wonderful Magical Words That Work – *Secrets to Create Permanent Success and Happiness*

Forever Cast in Endless Time

Bill Arnott

Silver Bow Publishing
720 Sixth Street, Unit # 5
New Westminster, BC
CANADA V3L3C5

Title: Forever Cast in Endless Time
Author: Bill Arnott
Cover Art: "November Beach" painting by Candice James
Layout and Design: Candice James
Editor: Candice James

All rights reserved including the right to reproduce or translate this book or any portions thereof, in any form without the permission of the publisher. Except for the use of short passages for review purposes, no part of this book may be reproduced, in part or in whole, or transmitted in any form or by any means, electronically or mechanically, including photocopying, recording, or any information or storage retrieval system without prior permission in writing from the publisher or a licence from the Canadian Copyright Collective Agency (Access Copyright).

Print 9781774031612
Epub 9781774031629

Library and Archives Canada Cataloguing in Publication

Title: Forever cast in endless time / Bill Arnott.
Names: Arnott, Bill, 1967- author.
Description: Poems.
Identifiers: Canadiana (print) 20210139951 | Canadiana (ebook) 20210139986 | ISBN 9781774031612
    (softcover) | ISBN 9781774031629 (EPUB)
Classification: LCC PS8601.R648 F67 2021 | DDC C811/.6—dc23

www.silverbowpublishing.com
info@silverbowpublishing.com
© Silver Bow Publishing 2021

To every dreamer, artist, and wanderer.

Contents

Black Sunset, Blurred Time ... 9
Murmuration ... 10
Forever Cast in Endless Time ... 11
Southwest Coast Path ... 12
Fire Flight: Haiku ... 13
At Horseshoe Bay ... 14
Impressionist Landscape, Culinary Sky ... 15
Bejeweled Skeleton ... 16
Night Sky ... 18
Yggdrasil ... 19
This Flight Tonight ... 20
Blank Canvas ... 21
Narsarsuaq Newlyweds ... 22
Lavender with Sky Blue Polka Dots (for JB) ... 23
Hit It ... 24
Lewis Chessmen ... 25
Falmouth in Bronze ... 27
Groove ... 28
Mayan Sunset ... 30
Weekend Party ... 31
Wordless Song ... 32
Lake (for JSJ) ... 33
The Guy Fawkes Inn ... 34
Portal ... 35
The Itsy-Bitsy Dream Catcher ... 36
Wander ... 37
Alchemy: Ekphrasis in Chalk ... 38
Alfred Wallis ... 39
Gobletful of Porthmeor Rock'n'Roll ... 41
Skull Cinema ... 43
Force Eight ... 44
The Allure of Sir Winston ... 45
Symphonic ... 47
Dave Went to California ... 48
Detail and the Deep Blue Sea ... 50
Freestyle Sunset (Jervis Bay, New South Wales) ... 51
After the Gig ... 52

Adrift ... 55
Armistice ... 56
Auntie Played the Piano ... 57
Beck: Home on Wheels (for KR & MR) ... 58
Camino, Clams, y de Compostela ... 60
Closing Bell ... 62
Edge of the World ... 63
Iain ... 64
Ogopogo ... 65
Auld Lang Syne ... 66
Elegy for Gord ... 67
Emerge ... 68
Acknowledgements ... 70
Author Profile ... 71

Black Sunset, Blurred Time

Pall sky, sun sets unseen,
but I know time,
more or less,
as crows take flight
eliminating day.

Against darkening backdrops,
I cluster and count:
two hundred,
five hundred,
one thousand,
until numbers thin, but don't end.
They never seem to end.

I follow their flight,
across city skyline,
broad dark swathes
en route to rookery homes,
nestled in suburban pockets
of towering cottonwoods.

Corvids bisecting time,
as they do, bending space continua
in fluid winking bands,
ushering Stygian chaperones
between days, and space,
enfolding the last of the light
in black sunset and blurred time.

Murmuration

5 pm, Friday, Seattle, 4th and Pine.
Pacific Northwest grey, late autumn.
Sunset slivers muscle through cast iron:
a sympathy card sky.

Then, out of nowhere,
an explosion of murmuration
overhead, ablaze, twisting, twirling
starlings in hundreds of thousands.

Fantasia flamenco swirls.
Nothing in nature could possibly occur
in this harmonic magnitude
without Attenborough.
Yet, here, between skyscrapers
it does occur, in swooping synchronization.

Rush-hour commuters, walkers, cyclists,
we all stop dead, a quarter million of us,
realizing we're witness — at this instant,
to the extraordinary and we stand, gawking skyward
to the likes of an alien invasion film,
when the mother ship descends
to blacken a metropolis sky.

Thousands of strangers united
in a colossal event beyond comprehension.
Bound inextricably. Mesmerized,
watching the symphonic sky formations.

Eventually, the swarm moves on,
tornado blur of iridescent black,
to dissipate, or not ... elsewhere.

The rest of us still stand staring skyward ...
eventually dissipate, move on.

Forever Cast in Endless Time

A draping swirl of matador cape,
the charge of changing season,
birdsong prescient as recess bells
circular chorus chime.

We run from
the bark of a starter gun,
shot echoes.

Landy shoulder-glances.
Gamblers' chits discarded,
tumbling,
whirlwind breezes,
sound of hamster wheel.

Runners circling in bronze,
forever cast in endless time.

Southwest Coast Path

Treading along the coastal path,
footsteps carry on
crunching shingle, pebble, strand
beside rock cliffs and dunes.

Golden scoops of silica.
Heaped desert on the beach.
Slicked-down marram blown askew
in need of cut or comb.

Rolling bluebells, heather, thrift,
foxgloves, fragrant gorse —
scent of summer, South Pacific,
ripened peach and coconut.

Heartbeat of a raven's wings
pumps through veins of wind,
penetrating jackdaw's gaze,
a solitary chough

Bay becomes a palette:
green, blue, aquamarine,
fired in a wash of sun,
extinguished by the rain.

Gusty squalls of spindrift
strafing salty spray.
Surf — a metered metronome,
percussion on the shore.

Cadence of the wind and waves,
pulsing melody.
Every step harmonic fugue
as the chorus carries on ...

Fire Flight: Haiku
Peachland, 2017

Sun setting crimson
toward treeline horizon
apocalyptic

Pines glowing ember
under crackling scarlet sky
shrouded in hot grey

Waves of bombers dive
jettison ochre payloads
splashing amber blood

All around fires burn
people fleeing from forest
desperate to be safe

Treed land, indiff'rent
burning above and below
as everyone runs

To where, no one knows
wondering if it will end
when the world is ash

At Horseshoe Bay
Baden Powell Trail: Deep Cove to Horseshoe Bay, August 2016

Four days of lonely mountain ridges, summits,
cutting through evergreen hollows,
surrounded in Emily Carr.

Dirt and rock and mud. At times, no trail at all
Judge and jury hung over my shoulder,
questioning being here.

Woodpecker knock, *(Come in!)*
amber icicle, resin scent,
pine nuts spit in soil,
muffled breeze, twig fingers,
thoughtful scratch, *I wonder*

Sagging boardwalk snakes through
checkerboard lakes and marsh,
the only path — this pockmarked patch
heaped with blueberry bear scat

Snap of branches to my right.
Movement behind me grows
to cracking boughs.
I call out ... no reply.

A bear! ... And I'm alone.
My mind races, paces.
Run or stay the course?

I continue on singing a wavering song.

At Horseshoe Bay
I contend with unmarked cliffs.
I scramble-slide,
from granite to cedar, hemlock, safety
eventually emerge, yelp victory.

Impressionist Landscape, Culinary Sky
Cézanne, Matisse—desert horizon, blurs of camouflage heat

By Dali's hand, crucified saguaro slumps, spiky cross,
life dissipates in pulpy drips
striking sand with momentary sizzles.
Madman, twisting moustache on the fly,
silent movie villain spies his wife, her lover,
smears oily lust on canvas.

Picasso's blue-rose-crystalline frontier,
suspended eyes — pared moon
and low-slung Venus
hung in velvet gloaming,
fluid brush tai chi, single stroke.
Pamplona streets turn to turbid labyrinth
preludes chaos, midday blood, *ole!*

Swirl of funnelled desert dirt,
lazy bouncing tumbleweed.
Lyric ball bounds across the screen,
whistles in a rising wind,
settling a Morricone score.

Vista: bowls, pyramids, ingredients of sunset sky.
Cumin, cayenne, cinnamon, chilli dusting hues,
nutmeg, saffron, turmeric. Suspend a stifled sneeze.

Above sautéed horizon, cast iron anvil cloud,
stewing, brewing storm explodes.
Lightning chiffonades dried foliage,
mustard ground left scorched:
obsidian, black serving glass
wrapped in canvas,
plated painted desert cassoulet,
simmering curry sky.

Bejeweled Skeleton
Northwest Cornwall, a mild Tuesday in March

Carbis Bay — Hayle Towans.
Waves wash, shucked oyster brine aroma.
Gannets glide, acrylic daubs in white.
Crushed bivalves underfoot.
Glint of stucco flecked with glass.
Cuttlefish and jellies, puddles of grape jam.

One thousand gritty, crunching miles
on tattered trail shoes.
Damp and ripened fleece
wafting whiffs of watery dog.
Fifty stretching pitches worth of sand
separating here from there.

Sudsy trim embroiders surf, tinged emerald.
Beach crimped in cobblestones,
treacle, amber, onyx.
Separated stainless sky, a rip through tattered clouds,
patched and sewn in topaz.

Charcoal caves face foreshore.
Hollow sockets stare,
seep foamy tears,
Silent, sightless sighs ...
what secrets have you witnessed?

I long to know
the story of the spectre ship,
having found its partial skeleton,
where crumbling granite cliff
and sandstone bleeding iron
front receding water.

Partially buried remains
emerge from shallow graves.
Metal rib, one shoulder blade

jut from pooling beach-corroded headstone,
afterthought wrapped in bull-kelp shawl.
Another type of seagrass, look of mermaid hair,
pigtail braided samphire, delicate green bow.

I've stumbled on a gift-wrapped grave.
Cemetery plot for foundered ship
murdered just offshore,
by storm and reef and negligence,
a century-and-a-half ago.

Succumbing in this stretch of sea,
these steely broken bones,
thrown ashore, thrust themselves
right here, chosen final resting place
a stone's throw
from sandcastle foundations.
Remaining until now.

Open ended mystery,
I'm left to wonder
what's being shared,
calling out
what am I meant to see
in this barnacle crusted bit of boiler?

Piece of tempered anchor.
Chunks of the forgotten,
resembling severed limbs
discarded by a tomb.

Night Sky
And I wonder if anything could ever feel this real forever?
***If anything could ever be this good again?** —Dave Grohl, Everlong*

From the end of a southwest branch line, lilting north,
reassuring pull of pack on my shoulders,
I walk along a beach from the train into town.
Night sky's alight — planets and stars,
dippers, Orion, the moon,
occasionally Venus and Mars on some nights.

Every celestial body's up there,
even downgraded Pluto.

Dave G himself would be wondrous
at what I hear as I cross High Street.
The majesty of a young foreign band
thrashing out a cover of his make-or-break song.

A nondescript pub
on the edge of the continent,
edge of the world, a place of people.
I so love that magic
I'm hard-pressed to find elsewhere,
Knowing I'm not alone, in this
keeps me coming back.

Under countless, nameless stars,
I thank you, whoever, whatever you are,
as a hero's soundtrack plays,
a dream right here ....
a dream I'm walking in now.

And I wonder if anything could ever feel this real forever?
If anything could ever be this good again?

Yggdrasil

Yggdrasil —
the world tree, mother ash
stands astride a Nordic knoll
beyond Uppsala's temples
where every god takes meat and mead
amongst the Norns —
Wyrd, Verðandi, Skuld.

Atop the tree, the eagle with no name resides
witness to our lives and spindle whorls of fate.
An eyrie shared with a hawk called *Veðrfölnir*,
witherer of wind.

When I saw the eagle, I was drifting on a wooden ark
in looming crags of crystal leaded ice.
'Nattoralik', whispered the Greenlander,
aurora eyes squinting into cloudless Arctic sky
following the nameless one in flight.

High overhead a giant sailed
across a canvas of Egyptian blue.
The hawk, invisible to us,
though its presence was felt
in the eagle's sweeping gaze.
Removing every trace of wind,
breath sucked silent from our lungs,
a contour feather — *whoosh* ...
the only sound.

This Flight Tonight

A hum of soft blue light
laps in gentle waves,
undulating on the cusp
of audibility.

Enfolded on a reclined seat,
thin padding custom shaped
to fit no human form,
I'm shimmied, beneath
a brightening blue,
near neon now,
wash that rises to a chop.

Beyond a porthole window
stars are humming past.
Same silent sound
as our internal blue,
launched like *Boney M*
aboard their *Night Flight to Venus*.

I close my eyes,
close the stars and the sky,
open my pocket of dreams
and hum along with *Nazareth*
on *This Flight Tonight*.

Blank Canvas
Inspired by George Dow's **Parade Street (East)**

Canvas, blank, hung at eye level.
A whitewashed mirror,
mirror on the wall,
reflecting everything and nothing.

What you see in your mind's eye,
a swirl of possibility, potential, creativity:
pastel, acrylic, oil.
Brushes dip, in gentle daubs
and slashing strokes.

Conductor in the pit, a parry-thrust baton
Our rainbow orchestra ignites,
excites the sensory,
to stimulate like Saturday TV:
Crazy tunes in technicolour runes
hurled as thunderbolts from Thor.
Electric art. Eclectic start and finish.
The unfinished ... finished.

Narsarsuaq Newlyweds
Inspired by an unmarked photo, southwest Greenland

Black and white photo
on black and white wall.
A wedding picture.
The two in the frame,
are not black and white.
Both white — around 1950,
between wars,
at this US Airforce outpost.
The newlyweds both beam.

He, in uniform, military cap
clasped beneath an arm.

She, in her uniform,
cascading lace.
bouquet gripped,
two-handed lifeline, or
an Oscar for best female
in a supporting role.

Happiness in their smiles,
make no mistake,
but in the eyes,
a ripple of uncertainty —
that quiver animals feel ...
before a seismic tremor.

Lavender with Sky Blue Polka Dots (for JB)

She wore her shirt like a protest.
Not the garment so much as how it gripped her.
An exclamation, as revealing of character
as it was a means of hiding physicality.

The fact she wore it one time
five days straight
alluded to much more.

Coordinated scarf tied anew each day —
knotted to the left,
knotted to the right,
in front, swept back,
and on day five a shoulder wrap:
a half size shawl,
a prideful shade of lavender
with sky blue polka dots.
A fragrant, drifting cloud.

I wondered if she could fly.

Hit It

Hokusai says ... pay attention, notice ... stay curious ... keep changing, you just get more who you really are. He says get stuck, accept it, repeat yourself as long as it's interesting. —Roger Keyes

A tire spins,
spits bits of loam
wet, yielding
fleeting traction,
quick transaction,
satisfaction.

Shoulda, coulda, woulda
put on chains,
drive through snow-blind night
and traffic lights,
illuminating puddles,
squishy footsteps,
umbrella husks in bins.

A touch of gas,
it spins and spins.

If only this would catch
we'd drop it into gear ...
be outta here.

Lewis Chessmen

Removed from the crowd
in a spotlight
with chessmen
granted visitation rights
in stagnant museum air.
Hospital hush
footfalls fade away
down vaulted marble corridor
dissipating echo of leather

Peering into lit glass, intrigued, bemused,
bent deep at the knee, I become a giant
beholding Lilliputian companions.

Glass walls dampen what's being said—
planning their subsequent play.

Any day now knight seems to say to bishop and pawn
we'll take cover behind a castle
escape when lights are out.

Bishop stifles a yawn, summons the will
to offer a placating smile,
I've waited this long he muses,
what's a thousand years more?

Given their odyssey:
cetacean to hunter, craftsman,
trader and merchant,
crossing Celtic Sea
to Hebridean outlier
en route to Liffey's Dark Pool.
Planted like ivory seeds
until harvested.
Plucked like potatoes
plated and served in the capital.
King and queen deadpan, above it,

despite being in the midst,
raised ever so slightly, in separate squares.

I can nearly touch carved toothy tusk
through glass, trace each tiny notch.

The polish of centuries
scouring sea salt scrub,
spindrift, sweat
and concentration.

The knight's now commanding
 another pawn that won't move.
Bishop's smile warms imperceptibly.
Knight exudes a silent *harrumph.*

No longer outsized,
I'm with them, among them,
pondering our next move
when I sense the return of soft leather
to stamp out this spotlight caesura
and haul me from this odyssey.

Falmouth in Bronze

A yawn from gaping Carrack Roads.
Little Falmouth gleaming proud here in Penryn.
Swirling cloud winks sunlight
into slowest pulsing strobe —
slate nimbus fat with rain — a glitter ball.
Rippled river, moving dance floor.

Swans self-aware, pair off, shake tails,
neck beak to beak, in alabaster hearts.

I cross the floor, hike mud around a headland
to the site of Mylor's hoard where sod and peat
spat Bronze Age weaponry and tools.
Patina gristle left to rot for centuries.
One's passed to me; I lift it up
with delicate white gloves:
four thousand years suspended in my palms.
Malachite, a shade of Asian jade,
alchemy from artisans
knapped in DNA and time.

I'm there, both here, and now.
A Tardis in this implement
I'm holding like my firstborn
cradled with a reverie I can't articulate
knowing I have held this once before.

Groove

Vinyl pirouettes, a needle touchdown:
groove, groove, groove.
Road grabs you in a bear-hug,
 highway getaway, asphalt bitumen
grooves, grooves, grooves,
and from the trunk the funky funk
of Mr T, Thelonious Monk,
Marsalis Boys play left and right.

Speakers installed in the rear
of a silver chrome thunderbird, my word!
The sound is crystal clear — treble, woofer,
double bass vibrates up, out, and through
Corinthian patent leather.

Headlights splay across a country roadway,
single lane both ways in
groovy grooves groovin'
to the smooth, smooth sounds of Billie Holiday,
Buddy Rich and Buddy Guy (every buddy, every guy)
Lady Ella too, (three, four) as Oscar takes the rougey baton-lead
on tickled ivories, black and pearly white ...
skip, hip-hop, span the jazz and blues
and rock n' roll in infancy across the delta blue,
through new orleans and kansas city
on to chi-town, up to harlem,
leap that pond, a mariana trench and one mighty
groove, groove, groove
to move the ocean.

Music, rhythm our giant orb
of oxygen and hydrogen.
This oily ball that
move, move, moves
to hot pressed tunes on fossil fuel 45s
and full length 33s

like seaside clifftops — Baja, Mazatlan,
needle dives toward an ocean groove
and all we need to do
to feel the heat of ocean beat
so cool, cool, cool
is be in that deep blue sea,
glissando, rondo, heartbeat music.

Everybody plays this single, shoreline shingle,
swooning tunes we scrunch along
in dancing shoes to upbeat a cappella company
in perfect, perfect harmony.

That's what we see:
a seaside bridging chorus,
chorusing our
groove, groove, groove ...

Mayan Sunset

A shudder of leaves in autumn gust,
each fibrous paddle volleys low slung sun.
Light-beams bounce from chlorophyll,
rustle onomatopoeic, wind-chime through flora,
shared intimacies, signing, deciduous jazz-hands,
I half expect roots and trunks to step and kick,
line dance away to something annoyingly catchy,
perhaps Sondheim or Sullivan,
then clap and laugh like no one's watching,
secretly hoping everybody is.

Heat hangs. Tomorrow should start chilled
I'll look for the box of sweaters,
something warm and comforting with just a hint of itch.
A hug. You pull on, push arms in, squeeze head through.

Turns out the chorus line is rooted, going nowhere.
Leafy little mirror greens, lacklustre now,
as fishing lures trolled too slow. There's life there still,
although no longer as attractive as they were.
Even peckish fish have grown disinterested,

Chime effect of breeze in green
has softened too and what I thought was hot
I now find temperate, agreeable,
like the slightly musty sweater
from the bottom of the pile.
Comforting, as sun slowly sets,
the world a wash of sentiment in crimson.

Weekend Poetry

Fingers hover.
Questioning
how much to reveal?

Rational voice does its best
to convince you
you won't fall,
reminding you where
safety, support resides.
A net, with nothing to fear in open mesh
but sincerity.

Breath held,
grip clenched,
you peer, beyond
the precipice, the plummet,
allow, force yourself,
to press ... send.

Wordless Song

Cradling guitar on hotel bed I feign the rockstar
with a resonating soulful strum — E minor.
Rumpled sheets, residual musk
layered on stacked pillows
complete the weary scene.

Perhaps it's just the lofty view, hangover, broken lamp
that resonate of glory days imagined
along with thickened tongue.
I sound uncannily like Tom Waits,
waiting for a wisp of germination,
sleeping muse now dormant
in suspended animation until it stirs ...

Outside ugly sleet's transformed —
now wondrous, crystalline
drifting downy, fluttering, flakes
through high rise glass.
A snow globe where life-size action figures
shuffle through their day
shoulders hunched to elements
under weighty whitened world, dampened city hushed.
Same off-white as tangled linen masking weathered mattress
Egyptian weave on acoustic bed-mate's curve stirs.

Uncertain tap, a rap incessant now,
ignoring *Do Not Disturb*
peering in, a pretty head, unexpected.

Rising taste buds, manifest creativity,
hourglass yearning, reaching copper lifelines,
tremulous touch relaxes, resonates, drawn close.
Caress harmonic chord, up tempo
matches dynamics, momentum
creating a perfect wordless song.

Lake (for JSJ)

An open expanse — watery in makeup,
a limitless lake
stretching out before you.

Effort brought you to this mostly rocky shore.
Patchy quicksand, tidal sinkholes
beckon *'at least moisten toes'*.

Exertion so great to reach this far.
You questioned yourself countless times,
yet here you are proud and terrified.

This intensity, new,
akin to razor-raised taste buds.
Water beckons, glints sun, ripples with whitecaps.

Beyond, and after that? Where water swallows sky?
Does it drop off? With cutting rocks and biting fish?

Echoes clutter, leave you feeling falsely less alone
despite an absence of others.

This lake, its vastness — colour you'd never fathomed,
in depthless fathoms, receding in journal scrawls ...
crumpled, torn, and tossed to ebbing tide.

Encroachment, dread, futility against the surge
as you scramble to sandbag retaining walls.

With a neap exhale
you return to *'proper'* pursuits,
to toil toward the next mile-marker, hopeful ...
but it's nowhere near this open body.

The Guy Fawkes Inn
Northumbria 2016

Seated:
in an ancient pub,
a high-back hardwood chair,
drink placed on ebony-stained table
with a wobble.

Contentment.
Distinguished, dark imperial pint of porter,
frothed in white,
reminiscent of Nelson Mandela
balanced ... on a tipsy punching clown.

Performance.
One-foot jazzy tap,
as I work to still the sway
that slowly loses relevance,
crescendos in satisfying swallows.

Now Knopfler mumbles far away
So Far Away, so true
so very far away from you,
from everywhere.

Still seated:
in an ancient pub,
a high-back hardwood chair,
drink placed on ebony-stained table
with a wobble ...
you have one more.

Portal
On take-off, a few thousand feet over Auckland

Through imitation glass, an imitation world removed,
observer and observed ... observing.
Real and imagined blur, in chalk-dust atmosphere.
The velvet sound of blackboard brushes dampened.

Tainted puffs of cumulous, a hint of pink.
A sunset, rare on blackened khaki earth.
A kiln in stone-fruit summer sky.
A harvest, cropped.

A threaded needle eyelet
cinched into a knot, snapped taut with teeth,
caught somewhere in between a grimace and a smile.

Through imitation glass
this imitation world slides by,
a curtain drawn in water droplets,
darkening to ashen-grey, to twilight-dusk
and finally ... to black

The Itsy-Bitsy Dream Catcher

Sun peers from horizon.
Sparrow's two-note song.
Day breaks, a promise of heat,
sensory start of summer.

Moist morning air:
jasmine, lilac.
Someone mows a lawn.
Crows carry on, conversing.

Outside our front door
something new unfolds.
Artisan architect webbing,
construction underway.

A structural frame takes form,
glinting silver, sunrise dew.
Subtlest vibrating thrum
of fly-tied fibres cinched in solidity.

A spin, a spindle, a strand:
knit, purl, reef and square.
Cloven hitches, granny knots
embroidered into a matrix.

Working toward a centre unseen,
an octet weave as one,
this trapping trapeze an open mouth net,
a yawning airborne weir.

Commenced, concluded, completed.
A hunter-gatherer space in time.
A catcher of dreams.
A trapper of animated edibles.

Wander

I think I could wander this way the rest of my life—a small knapsack, sneakers, an old Navy CPO shirt, khaki pants, a small knife, a bottle opener, a nail clipper, a pencil & pad, a book, all I have —Lawrence Ferlinghetti, Writing Across the Landscape

Pull of pack on shoulder.
Obligatory hug, assuring, reassuring strain.
A tethered thread of DNA,
taut hawser to the shore,
familiar tidal ebb and flow. Familial.

Weigh the anchor.
Cast off, if/when, you dare.
Take care, to dodge the crap
laid down, piled high, for you
and any passers-by.

It gets into your hikers' grooves
where nothing gets it out,
except passing time.
Emptying, clear-mind clarity,
and grit from scuffled, shuffled, miles walking,
walking away, away ...
toward something else,
an imagined something better,
something new from tattered clothing
dropped into a roadside bin.

Don't look too far into the depths,
or dark sewn patches
where reality resides.

A solitary burnt-out star
trails comet-like across crepuscular rays
disturbing a reticent sky.

The crunch of well-worn shoes on gravel fades away.

Alchemy: Ekphrasis in Chalk
Inspired by the carvings of Pradeep Gade

Soft stone, a palette porcelain,
in cylinders of white.
Scribbles, scrapes
on black-green board.

Students stare toward summer,
spring erased in puffing clouds
from brushes beaten.
Afterwards, a solitary stick
of dusty stone ... potential.

Just inside exterior,
beneath the surgeon's blade,
incise, carve redundancy away,
dispatched in dustings of new life:
a leaf, a building.

Beyond the confining classroom walls,
artisans, like me, keep company,
outside, where life occurs
in art and sculpture,
in dreams, in dusty puffs
of cloud and creativity.
Potential realized, at last.

Alfred Wallis

I drop to a knee, graveside.

Behind me blue-green water
thrashes an unseen reef,
with granite stacks
and blackened blocks of basalt,
sending streamers strafing skyward,
towering ivory ribbons,
splashing frothy white,
reversing ocean-liner celebration
drifting driving out to sea.

The grave I'm kneeling at, home to one
who never knew celebrity, alive,
now has a name in certain circles.
Artists, painters, connoisseurs,
lovers of *The Craft*,
who may/may not know what they like,
idolize the man lying beneath ...
almost certainly turned to dusty calcium,
no trace of flesh, hair long gone.

There is no glamour in the ground.
No glamour beneath six feet
of earth compacted peat
and compressed sod
long since laid to rest.

Alfred Wallis
lies under my bended knee.
The painter who pursued his art,
when no one seemed to care,
painting water, boats and life:
the manner that he knew ...
genius in a childlike eye.

That's what I love about this man of depth.
We know him well and yet so little.
Uncomplicated to a fault.
Brushstrokes now over-analysed
beyond the point of reason.

A man who simply loved to paint
and painted love as well
in water, boats and seaside views
like what's behind me now.

Gobletful of Porthmeor Rock'n'Roll

Sandy shoreline joining pincer-points of land —
a rocky crab-claw grasping at the Atlantic.
Limpets, whelks and cuttlefish-bone
litter a wave-tamped shore
with discs of slate like Lilliputian blackboards

Sun set some time ago.
I shuffle through the black angled slope of beach
a line of breaking waves, my guide.
Something's different this evening, in their sound ...
a noise like throwing countless dice
at walls in shadowed lanes.

Each rising surge of water
tumbling on the shore tonight
is spinning fist-sized rocks
like Stone Age chorus lines.
Rows of Neolithic dancers
kicking with the tide; their score —
the roar of wind and wave, their band —
the sea and shore.

These walking rocks, a rolling stroll,
the sound surrounds me all around.
Somewhere a Bronze-Age man, my age,
smiles at the symmetry.
When he was here more land was near.
Sea was lower, far away.

Where Guinevere was lost to Lancelot,
and he besot with her,
beseeched his men for freedom,
ran the sand from Camelot,
beyond the end of land
where Perceval, and every knight,
at last, when done, could rest.
Each wayward haggard wanderer

returned to Scilly's barrows abandoned,
chalice boxed, in someone's attic.

Finally, at peace, like you, like me,
and all we see or long to be,
on nights like this — at one —
ensconced in endless, darkened sea.

Skull Cinema
***The path is made in the walking of it.* —Zhuangzi**

A film unwinds with the soft spinning hum
of reel to reel and continues:
Images, memories flicker and fold.
An origami dance in 2D:
dusted mercurial, gathered and spliced,
revealed on a wide cinemascope screen.

Dream-sown thoughts woven in needlework
are spindled, spun, knotted and purled
and sewn into tapestries
hung from a wide cinemascope screen.

Footfall arteries, pulse of a tide,
cadence primordial,
ECG paces, left to the right,
trail on a wide cinemascope screen.

Each stride a vignette a chapter, a verse.
The journey a palette imagined ...
Producer, director and writer
converge to merge
on a wide cinemascope screen.

Stories we walk into, through and around
burst into kernel-pop thoughts:
remembered, real-time, lived and relived
on a wide screen.

A film unwinds to the contented tail-wag
— *thwip-thwap* —
of light on a wide white screen ...
then stops.
Skull Cinema over.

Force Eight

Aboard a pilot cutter, *Abigail,*
fifty-four feet of wind-powered teak,
reinforced steel, struts, strakes and keel,
we race ahead of force eight the gale on our tail.
Heaving up and heaving over twelve-foot heaving swells
that break in icy froth of spindrift strafing my face:
saline sting of airborne surf, buckshot cut on skin,
whipped water — black and blue to white —
beaten, tethered lifeline, cleats deck-tacked,
sufficient play to make my way midship to stern.

Our huddled hands hang on. Waves thrash.
Submerged by half, our ship diminished.
Merciless Atlantic, Celtic Sea
then the storm subsides followed by
penetrating calm, grounded, finally rounding home.

Above, beyond, hang herring gulls,
fixed wing as kites, while gannets plummet,
suicidal gold tipped meteors smashing in the sea.

Later, in the style of Polaroid film,
blurred memories emerge, in chevron wake.
A storm-riled ocean chased by rage.
The gale gripping mane-like crests.
We ride each plunge of bowsprit ...
a harpoon spearing plankton-sparkled waves
through endless, endless night.

The Allure of Sir Winston

Somewhere in London,
alone amongst eight million,
stands a dark-wood Edwardian pub ... *Sir Winston*.
White painted exterior timber and beams,
geraniums hanging like plump ruby earrings.
One door, ajar, beckons me ... enter.

I proceed inward, stooping slightly under lintel,
enjoying a moment of feeling overly tall.
Inside the pub, a long chocolate coloured bar
lacquered in a century of spit and elbow polish,
generations of spilled beer and saturated smoke.

Taps of every colour run the bar length,
are thrust like spikes and studs into the counter:
bitters, ales, IPAs, and ESBs and stouts
while porters bookend ciders.

Along the floor
a scuffed brass rail resembles anklets,
hammered straight, snapped free
from anchor ball-and-chains.
This place could be a thrift store,
or an old-world antique shop.
Teapots, model planes, railways,
tennis racquets, piggy banks.

And every type of instrument:
flutes, drums, and clarinets,
violins and saxophones
squeezeboxes, banjos,
baritones, even a sousaphone
hanging from the ceiling,
the only dusting ever
must be when punters sneeze.

And now I've pissed off Andy Capp,
standing by the seat I've chosen.

This tiny ancient man in ancient tweed,
huffs despite a row of empty stools.
I've clearly chosen *his*.

I take the low road and ignore him
immerse myself in an imperial pint,
snap newspaper in front of me,
international sign for Do Not Disturb.

A further awkward pause ...

Andy lets out one last huff
while I pretend to understand
the cricket scores.

Symphonic

Not delivery
but instead that nano-micro instantaneous
    flash
when something's something new.

Deity, alchemy, necromancer Botticelli's Venus
birthed astride an open-hulled shore-bound shell.
Westerlies swirling locks.
The colours of salmon, sand and spring
    — printemps — adrift.
No pilots, gigs, ushers in sight,
just the tug of instinct, artisanal tide
with widespread beckoning world.

A beach
where houngans, mambo, druids
palette-armed rest in ex-postdiluvial spectrums.
Egg-yolk concoctions, imagined,
emerge, dripping from sea-lapped rock
to the molar-grind of mussels,
grit and clench of coital conclusions.

Symphonic, the slow, slow applause of oysters.
An orchestra, balconied scallops, clams in a pit.
Waves wash, conduct, dissolve, for now
in splashes of harmonic steam.

Dave Went to California

Dave heard the song
first time he crossed the border.
I-5, California bound, no money, none,
save for a Shell card "borrowed" from his mom.
His car a loaner too.
The card enough for gas, slim-jims, egg muffins
and an endless pour of styro-tepid-coffee.
Zeppelin II and IV his company
for Californian pilgrimage.

There and back, four days ...
an aching in his heart.

Day one and two Zep II.
Day three and four Zep IV.
Four sticks, the ciggie slim-jims keeping company
with Bonham fills of tom-tom, coffee, petrol.

Four days; his misty mountain redwood hop
past Monterey across Golden Gate,
where ghostly haunts of undead Ferlinghetti,
Grateful Dead, and Journey echo.

Ins-and-outs of intercourse and interstates,
the off-and-on of off-ramps,
turnpike turnarounds,
an endless spin of wheels, squeals,
rubber laid in truck-stop bathroom stalls,
like rain-slick squalls.

Dave is heading north again,
and in the backseat a 24 flat of Pabst,
two jerry cans before the Shell card's cancelled.
The final day Dave knows
he'll get no coffee, fuel, refill,
and there's nothing left to eat.
No worries he's been here before, too often,
He'll survive just like his rifle toting dad.

And mom – long suffering mom –
will welcome him and cook for him
and send him on his way;
then check the post box ...
wait for her new Shell card to arrive.

Detail and the Deep Blue Sea
But the way to tame the Devil is not to go down there to the church and listen to what a sinful mean fool he is. No, love the Devil like you love Jesus: because he is a powerful man, and will do you a good turn if he knows you trust him. —Truman Capote

I slid into that space, again, a comfy purgatory —
prone, eyes cast upon a sky
where gulls and blue and cloud collide.
Adrift, as one, a-sail as sheets
and lines and knots align
and atmospheric surf breaks free.

A spirit wave, rises, curls, and rolls
to toss me, in this state, side to side.
The pulse of tide and nautiluses drift, drifting, adrift.
A forked expanse of blue, of you, of me, of sky, of sea
and all around this round of heaven, earth and water glow,
reflecting in our eyes.

Each pulse, a pull of saline stinging, singing.
The shoreline a scalloped stairway, samphire,
sand and grind of mollusc, mussel, oyster, clam.
The colour of a thin blue line, above, below,
dividing, joining, here and there, present, past,
as you and I cast off.

Our company:
a two-toned hue of open sky,
the detail, and the deep blue sea.

Freestyle Sunset (Jervis Bay, New South Wales)
We speak of course of that narrow strip of land over which the ocean waves and moon-powered tides are masters—that margin of territory that remains wild despite the proximity of cities or of land surfaces modified by industry. —W.J. Dakin, Australian Seashores

I drift, the direction of sleep,
sound of surging sea, set to birdsong score —
rooftop ruckus harmony, cacophony,
staccato squawks, a whizzing gliss,
cappella chirps on bee-bop peeps
with whippoorwill whines,
lorikeet prides in seven bands.

Glitter floats and dance halls
dressed in hanging mirror balls,
spinning, radiating lightness,
chorusing avian close encounters.

Extra-terrestrial melody
sung to a sun submerging,
settling into simmering ocean swells
and still, the sail-like sweep
of setting rainbow ...
sings, sings, sings.

After the Gig

Relaxed, reclined in armrest rows of padded seats,
our sleepy ferry creeps toward a sunrise.

Michael and I softly strum guitars.
Yes, I'm permitting myself to be *that* guy.
Accoustic call-and-answer starts our day
with aroma of fried bacon, crisp,
five cups of drip roast breakfast blend
lingering on clothes.

Ahead, Bowen Island, a child's likeness of a whale
all that's missing is the arcing waterspout
and one, humongous eye.

Beyond, inverted Vs of mountain blues and greens,
A confectioner's dusting of new snow
vertically mirrors a widening wake,
A whitewash skein tracing our trail
on ever calming teal.

Ah, Michael's tuned to open G,
a dampened banjo sound,
to share a song he just composed
somewhere on forest beach in Haida Gwaii.
Diminished chords, an echo of old growth,
how he conveys a people, place, the past
in single, resonating fifths remains a mystery.

Cast in icy canvas views,
we're cozy in our toques and scarves.
Muted patter, morning sounds surround.
Windows offer vista jolts of Kodachrome.
Last night dwindles like a murmur:
candlelit lounge, raised patrons,
at high tops, sipping winter cordials.

A cluster of our own —
poets, storytellers, singers mingled in the mix,
patted backs and hugs, laughter, barks, applause,
a clump of lushes pile on, despite the odds,
leave the bar as fans of poetry, and us.

After, crossing town,
in intermittent under-wattage streetlight,
adrenaline still staving off the cold, and wet,
I unfold my palm, two neatly folded twenties
and a five in hand — the evening's pay.
A police cruiser speeds onto a side street, red and blue.
Leaves me to wonder
who's life has changed forever.

Back "home" at the crash pad stacked-up house
welcoming artists, middle-aged land surfers
swim the living room sea,
catch sofas as they rise and fall
on swells and tidal surge,
ridden over rocky reef and shoal.

We sleep like drunken, hairy babies,
on thin sheets and pillows never changed,
happy just to have a place indoors.
Hot food, and wine; from the kitchen
wafts a warming apple crumble.

No tabs for the talent, cash only,
just like cover charges at the door.
I pulled a fist of coins from my jeans' pocket,
got on with a night of come what may and openness.

A chorus of my spoken-word recycles in a loop.
I let it circle, play harmony of poetry
and lifelong goals realized
on cold dark nights and ferry rides
that cross a stretch of inland sea.

Island refugees, weeknight drunks and poets
merge in dim-lit pubs to read, recite, resuscitate
and commit to sharing honesty.

Finally, stepping down, off my pedestal stage,
a striking woman, age inappropriate
haemorrhaging daddy issues, intercepts,
holds my gaze tells me that I'm "genius".

I decide I must be somewhere else,
but linger, just for a moment, then move on
to my home, not the sofa-house crash-pad
but the *real* home I return to,
imagining warm cinnamon and apple.

Adrift
I felt adrift, and slightly abandoned, in a new place (when travelling, this experience is partly euphoric, partly terrifying, and partly lonely) —Dave Bidini, *Midnight Light*

Airborne.
Afloat, a snow-clad mountain sea,
an heirloom quilt of water, field, humanity
where high rise hammered tent pegs
stake out property, unceded.

To the south, a vulcan peak stands solitary,
cascade cousin waiting to erupt.
Familial isolation, lava flow
towards a murky river
cutting through vermillion tape.

Recorders hidden deep in vases
filled with tiptoed tulips.
Tiny Tim falsetto, waiting to erupt.
A single mentos in a Pepsi can-can.
Devastating landscape portrait
of a family, posed, and poised.

Jet stream clings to the curvature of earth.
A photo singes ... corners curl
from sepia to ash.

Armistice

Injected, pierced through pinhole.
Red arterial glint of minted coins.
Lustre of used canes
and shiny new prosthetics.

Lion's mane,
in crimson bloom
on camouflage,
reveals what's inside.

Supporting crutch.
In lines no longer.
Row on row,
bent steel.

A partial cross of silver.
Nickels, dimes, quarters
dropped in a poppy can.

Auntie Played the Piano

Auntie played the piano,
where it patiently sat,
beneath the coat of arms
and heavy, heavy tapestry
of woven reds and golds.

The hanging tapestry
always struck her
as an ode to autumn.
The season and the sound alike
was what she liked;
and while she'd undulate in silent reverie,
Auntie struck the keys: each half note,
quarter, eighth, arpeggio, an almost slap
as though assaulted, an affront.

The little harpsichord that could
had best be kept in line,
lest Auntie dole a proper thrashing.

Concentration fixed of face,
arthritis vanishing
from knuckles suddenly supple.
A spinster soloing,
and solely for herself it seemed.
Her eyes would close, invariably,
while she would play,
her head at times asway
as though entranced.

Auntie played the piano,
beneath the fraying coat of arms
and heavy, heavy tapestry,
in autumn reds and golds.

Beck: Home on Wheels (for KR & MR)

I live in the space of a plus sized closet:
A closet set on wheels. Mobile. Home.
My own four papered walls,
on wheel-wells and axles.

I have flipped for greater clearance,
outbound trails, logging roads,
boondoggling in Walmart parking lots
and campsites with full hookups.
Water. Sewer. Power ...
Power of the open road.
Of freedom. Opportunity.

At times, a touch of loneliness,
but nothing I can't beat
with a good meal.

An oven mitt in peachy pink,
I keep next to the sink,
beside a colander.
The kettle, dish soap and a sponge,
all set beneath my pride and joy
— a poster — paper on the paper
in a rainbow orchestra of colour ...
      and Beck.

He talks to me, at times,
on the longest stretches of road
where static is the only channel
on the AM/FM; and we laugh,
commiserate and cry.

He laments *Soy un perdedor*,
and I say, "Don't be absurd!"
On the sectional,
the beach bag still holds sand
from west coast overnights.

The stereo tucked neatly in a cabinet,
its wires leading nowhere.
Life-support long severed, flatlined,
while a dreamcatcher
hangs stoically, angelically ...
above it all.

Each day, methodically,
I check the net,
imagine I'm a fisherman,
certain I can almost catch
a glimpse of adipose.

Of course,
no net can hold a dream;
but I still see a tailfin,
shades of whale white
in LP shades he wears so well.

Meanwhile, two bananas
just keep ripening.
The candle shrinks
progressively.

We'll have a solitary bake-off by the fire
or the auto centre of the big box retail store.

And I say solitary,
even though it's two of us,
because, really,
we're both ...
alone.

Camino, Clams, y de Compostela
St Michael's Mount to St James Grave

I climb a hill, in old snow crust,
expired, soured, beyond.
Below, a crescent, tinted, sand-dune beach,
in almond husk hues that bend and stretch,
forever discarded to March elements.
A chill to permeate eider, wool and ligaments,
beneath old soles.

A blend of mud and ice-skimmed loam,
the way of pilgrims, slipping, sinking.
A blinking, hoodwinked eye on a signpost
glancing ever east, like Sauron,
as the hobbits near, and Saruman lets everybody down.

A redhead rides a painted clamshell,
as a great saint crosses west Galicia,
home to Guthred, for a spell,
before more infidel, maverick moors moved in.

Broken, oaken booze-soaked casks
still wheeze beneath a thumbnail moon
and distant shores curved like prayer mats.

Behind me, a dragon-slayer's mount.
Celtic crosses, circled Druid stones.
A slosh of pious feet echoes
like an invocation.
The sound of footsteps,
balls on abacus,
the copper taste of corpses
and of promises reneged,
across a clamshell eye they roll.

Snow's long gone from Michael's Mount
and Ararat's as dry as
sun-bleached crucifixion bone.

But here, in Costa Verde Spain,
language, land and pintxos
rally from behind
and defeat the continental church
and currency in penalty kick shootouts.

Running from the field, the bulls,
these blisters buried in my boots
now seep Rioja red.

I cross myself and mutter *inshallah*,
remove my dusty shoes,
a money changer's belt, suspenders,
toss away a weathered mat and carry on.

Blurred in wind, Atlantic mist,
the color, scent of westward Avalon ...
a reminiscent whiff of history,
of saline, sandstone battlements,
and sea.

Closing Bell
Why, why so many roads, so many hostile citadels?
What did I take from so many markets? —Pablo Neruda, *Extravagaria*

Crenellated fortress walls,
takeovers, knights in black and white
no longer on a checkered board
with royalty.

Instead, on steeds
of surging market highs and lows,
a Lipizzaner sea, weapons of war
siege engines, lost crusades,
paperless trails to holy lands
elusive, votive offerings
to long dead gods.

The odds we play on trading day.

A ticker passes, passes by.
Now off you jesters, minstrels, bards
and leave me to my misery.

My wilting flower, drooping.

Pray the hurt and loss
and heartache disappear
before the lasting echo
of a closing bell
has rung.

Edge of the World
North Beach, Haida Gwaii, shadows of eagles and ravens

A sandy swath, horizon curve, beached star.
A fire-engine pylon crimson,
shave-cream daubs of surf and sky converge.

Land's edge, refracting sea,
a gorgonzola moon cinched taut
in double Windsor-knot of samphire.

Polished pieces, purple glass,
one single winking eye rinsed out.
Washed in from just beyond that blur
where cumulous and Lipizzaner rollers merge —
the word impossible in English,
known through yellow cedar heritage.

The People,
carved in growth-ring moieties.
Edge of the world, this rippled shoreline,
terra incognita, incognito,
peach-hued wake
of long-set solar energy,
enshrouded in a clear-cut gap.

Evergreen wrap, no longer *ever.*
No longer *green,*
No longer on the cusp ...
of anything.

Iain

We didn't stay in touch
after we were teens.

I heard he lived on the Island,
found a job in Creative.

While the rest of us hunkered safe in school,
Iain pursued his craft ...
and heroin.

Iain was always Dungeon Master
when we played D&D:
creating fantasy,
visualizing another world,
different ... maybe better.

One day
only one of us walked away
from fantasy role-playing, dice rolling
and daring the devil to chase us.

I hope Iain survived staying up,
devouring challenging books,
creating fantasy,
pursuing his craft ...
and heroin.

Ogopogo

On a lake view hill
polka dotted in sunflowers,
monsters nowhere to be seen,
no tourists passing through
to mistake curl of wake
as something else.

On that lake view hill,
I kissed a girl
falling in preteen love.

A few days later
she said, *'You're too nice'*,
leaves me for a bad boy
who'll do time
and leave child-rearing
to teenage her.

On a lake view hill
tourists passing though
report a sighting

Auld Lang Syne

Predawn, through frost,
a blossom blooms.

Bluebills clump,
in raptor eclipse,
under stone-fruit sky.

Light, dark,
auld lang syne,
hummingbirds and blossoms
lined up as witnesses ...

An oncologist tells Tom
... three to six.

Elegy for Gord
Don't tell me what the poets are doing / those Himalayas of the mind
—Gord Downie

Scribbled scripture,
tragic and hip.
A country mourns its saviour,
touring, carrying crosses
on which we weep,
bowed to wailing walls of marshalls,
penetrating dark, cellular solenoids
raised in vigil and tribute.

Futile candle-lit palette of hope
through haloed haze conjoined.
A fanning wash of laser strobes in concert,
shared universe and constellations.

Driven chords.
Three shores of sound and land
immersed, traversing tidal waves
in prose and balladry,
in conversant and connective
common score.

Memory, emotion,
lain like fronds
on roads to a kingly town.
Salvation sought in stereo,
black-tee disciples breaking bread
through strength of song, prayer,
desperate to drown the beating sound
of hooves, approaching ... passing.

Emerge
A true artist is not one who is inspired, but one who inspires.
—Salvador Dali

We sit, most nights on a sofa,
slouched in our inner sanctum,
where creativity resides,
then hides at times, as lights ignite
and bills insist on getting paid,
and we pay all our attention to that
instead of following
heart, inspiration, artist creativity.

Remember the prisoners Michelangelo saw,
those ethereal drifting figures
set in stone,
imprisoned
in the Academia
across the Arno, Adriatic.

We all are artisans and artists,
inspiration in our grasp
set just beyond this moment,

A ticking clock this lump of clay,
awaiting artistry and inspiration.

I grab hammers, chisels,
don an apron and compose.
Two righteous brothers sing
as clay gets moistened,
turns and fingers lock, unlock.

A buried muse, the fuse is lit,
to spark and burn
toward a finished product
yet to be revealed.

Clay rises, yields,
emerges from the kiln.

This piece, now glazed,
extends a hand, a smile,
nods toward its sculptor,
crafter,
our creator ...
that's the artist!

Each of us
inspiring and inspired
— carry on —
awaiting our next inspiration
   to emerge.

Acknowledgements
The following poems were previously published:

'Iain' *Down in the Dirt Magazine, Scars Publications, 2019.*
'Ogopogo' *Big Pond Rumours Magazine, 2019.*
'Auld Lang Syne' *The MOON Magazine, 2019.*
'Black Sunset, Blurred Time' *Eskimo Pie Magazine, 2019.*
'Fire Flight: Haiku' *Heartwood*, League of Canadian Poets, 2018.
'Murmuration' *Literary Yard Journal, 2019.*
'Impressionist Landscape, Culinary Sky' *Literary Yard Journal, 2019.*
'South West Coast Path' *Dawntreader Magazine, 2019.*
'Bejewelled Skeleton', *Literary Yard Journal, 2019.*
'Yggdrasil' *Plum Tree Tavern Magazine, 2019.*
'Blank Canvas' *The Ekphrastic Review, 2019.*
'Narsarsuaq Newlyweds' *Continuum, 2020.*
'Lavender with Sky Blue Polka Dots (for JB)' *Eve of St Ives*, UK, 2019.
'Hit It' *The Ekphrastic Review, 2019.*
'Lewis Chessmen' *Eskimo Pie Magazine, 2019.*
'Falmouth in Bronze' *Literary Yard Journal, 2019.*
'Groove' *Stereo Stories, 2020.*
'Mayan Sunset', *Eskimo Pie Magazine, 2020.*
'Weekend Poetry' *Eskimo Pie Magazine, 2020.*
'Wordless Song' *Eskimo Pie Magazine, 2020.*
'Lake (for JSJ)' *The Eunoia Review, 2020.*
'The Guy Fawkes Inn' *Dawntreader Magazine, 2020.*
'Portal' *The Ekphrastic Review, 2020.*
'The Itsy-Bitsy Dream Catcher' *New Reader Magazine, 2019.*
'Wander' *New Reader Magazine, 2019.*
'Alchemy: Ekphrasis in Chalk' *The Ekphrastic Review, 2019.*
'Alfred Wallis' *Literary Yard Journal, 2020.*
'Gobletful of Porthmeor Rock and Roll' *Literary Yard Journal, 2020.*
'Skull Cinema' *Literary Yard Journal, 2020.*
'The Allure of Sir Winston' in *Literary Yard Journal, 2020.*
'Dave Went to California' *Stereo Stories, 2020.*
'Detail and the Deep Blue Sea' *Quadrant Magazine, 2020.*
'Freestyle Sunset (Jervis Bay, NSW)' *Quadrant* Magazine, 2020.
'After the Gig' *The League of Canadian Poets, 2019.*

Author Profile

Author, poet, songwriter Bill Arnott is the bestselling author of *The Gamble Novellas*, award-winning travelogue *Gone Viking: A Travel Saga*, *Dromomania*, and the illustrated all-ages novella *Allan's Wishes*. His work is published in Canada, the US, UK, Europe, Asia and Australia and his column *Bill Arnott's Beat* is a feature in magazines around the globe. Bill's been awarded for prose, poetry, songwriting and for his eight year *Gone Viking* trek has been awarded a Fellowship at London's Royal Geographical Society. When not trekking the planet with a small pack, journal, and laughably outdated camera phone, Bill can be found on Canada's west coast, making friends and misbehaving. Join *Bill's Artist Showcase* newsletter for fun interviews and updates, or find Bill at: billarnottaps.wordpress.com | @billarnott_aps

www.ingramcontent.com/pod-product-compliance
Lightning Source LLC
Chambersburg PA
CBHW031228110526
44590CB00035B/3341